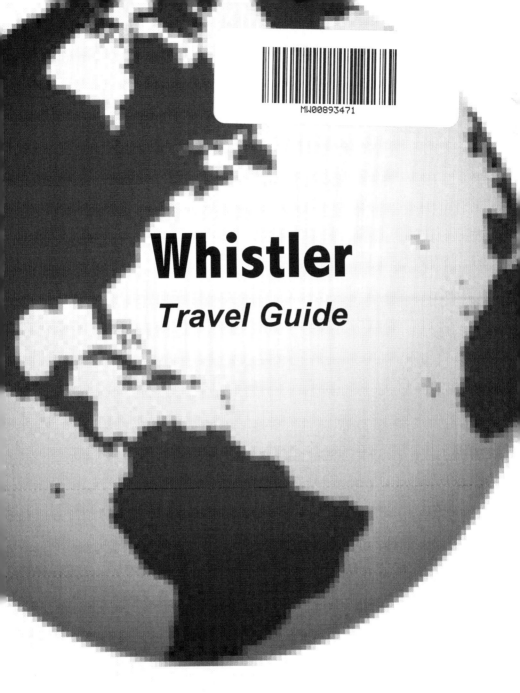

# Whistler

## *Travel Guide*

*Quick Trips Series*

# Table of Contents

# KNOW BEFORE YOU GO    48

## Whistler, B.C.

If you are looking for a world-class wintersports location in western Canada then Whistler, British Columbia is your ticket. This Winter Olympics location is a scenic mountain area with snowy winters yet moderate temperatures. Visitors return here year after year.

# WHISTLER TRAVEL GUIDE

The small mountain community has a passion for protecting and conserving the natural environment and it retains an international feel. Whistler has a diverse natural environment with rocky mountain peaks, ancient forests and glacier-fed rivers, streams and lakes making this a location that is both stunning and awe-inspiring.

As per the 2011 Canadian census, there were 9824 year round residents with two million visitors per year. On peak holiday weekends, the population can swell to over 55,000, opposed to 1975, when fewer than 1000 people lived in Whistler.

It takes 13,500 employees during the busy season to keep this hotspot running. Nearly half the population at Whistler is 25 to 34 year olds who are highly educated with 29 percent having a university degree.

# WHISTLER TRAVEL GUIDE

It is a family friendly destination as 20 percent of all households in Whistler have children who are enrolled in the three schools located within the valley. Because this is a family-friendly destination, Whistler has introduced WiFi hotspot, for a rental fee of $5 per day (plus a refundable deposit) you can eliminate roaming charges by connect up to 10 devices at a time; available at the Whistler Visitor Centre. 4299 Blackcomb Way, Whistler, BC, Canada 1-604-966-5500

Before ski lifts and snowboarders and even before the nineteenth century trappers and loggers, the Squamish and Lil'wat First Nations used the isolated valley for gathering and hunting. Bears (black and grizzly) and cougars, deer, rabbits and rodents, birds including the eagle, and fish all call this valley home. The marmot (a rock-dwelling rodent about the size of a small dog) is how Whistler got its name as this animal warns others of potential dangers by releasing a high-pitched whistle. Their calls can be heard, usually during the warmer seasons, throughout the mountains.

In 1914, Alex Philip opened Rainbow Lodge (used for fishing and as a holiday camp). Later that same year, the Great Pacific Northwestern railway pressed over the valley making a path to Prince George. In the late 1940's, Rainbow Lodge became a popular honeymoon spot but was only accessible by train or float plane (still a viable option for travel to Whistler) until the hydro road was paved in 1966.

The ski area was opened by the Garibaldi Lift Company and in 1968 Whistler held the Winter Games. Since then,

# WHISTLER TRAVEL GUIDE

Whistler has been known as a magnet for skiers and snowboards alike enjoying two of the highest ski mountains in North America. Blackcomb Mountain rises 1609 metres (5280 feet) and Whistler Mountain rises 1530 metres (5020 feet).

Whistler is the first designated resort municipality in Canada and was incorporated on September 6, 1975. 9 years after officially opening the village, December 1980, Whistler was ranked one of the top-notch resort destinations in the world. Similar in appearance to Vail Village in Colorado, Whistler's foundation was created by the same architect, Eldon Beck. The pedestrian village is actually built on an old garbage dump.

The main modes of transportation around the resort are carpooling, transit, walking or biking and 96 percent of seasonal residents use these modes on a regular basis, even in the winter. Transit was introduced to Whistler in 1991 and has the highest ridership per service hour in all of British Columbia. Day passes for an adult are $7.00 and $5.00 for students and seniors. There are also free bike parking racks installed throughout Whistler Village, the Upper Village, Whistler Creek and in parks from April to October. The village is linked by a pedestrian-only causeway called the Village Stroll that is lined with shops, restaurants and hotels.

# ☯ Customs & Culture

Whistler was designated as the 2009 Cultural Capital of Canada with painters, sculptors, ceramicists, multi-media artists, writers, actors, playwrights, photographers and filmmakers all calling this glacial mountain area home.

# WHISTLER TRAVEL GUIDE

Every year the Whistler Film Festival is held with thousands of people flocking to places like the Maurice Young Millennium Place that has a 250-seat theatre and a rotating art exhibition in the Scotia Creek Gallery. 4335 Blackcomb Way, Whistler, BC, Canada V0N 1B4 1-604-935-8410 www.myplacewhistler.org

Whistler has an outstanding art program that includes the Street Banner Art Program where local artists create unique banners to be hung on the light posts around the village.  Each series is displayed for two seasons and then sold to the public with revenues extending to future public art projects.

When visiting, stop by the Squamish-Lil'wat Centre for a history in culture regarding the two heritages and traditions of the people.  You'll see artifacts, art, carvings and tools that are similar and different to the two native

groups. And don't miss a story-telling session; they run at

regularly scheduled times. The on-site café has some

unique spins on contemporary foods like the venison chili.

The cost of visiting this excellent interpretive center is $18

and they are open daily from 9:30 am to 5 pm.

Squamish-Lil'wat Centre 4584 Blackcomb Way, Whistler,

BC V0N 1B0 1-866-441-7522 www.slcc.ca


There are approximately 16 art galleries and 10 studios

were you can practice or learn to basket weave, do

pottery, dance and many other forms of art. There are 12

local arts & cultural groups for people of all ages ranging

from writers groups and chorus to festival societies.

Whether you are an avid art collector, enthusiast or you

just want to admire some amazing work, a great way to

see all the local art at Whistler is to take a self-guided tour where each piece of art is identified with signs and

additional information can be accessed via phone or QR

code. Brochures about this walking tour are available at

Whistler Visitor Centre.

In 2008, an economic impact study was conducted that

centred on arts, culture and heritage. The study revealed

that the combined annual income of arts organizations

and artists in the Sea-to-Sky Corridor was an

unbelievable $16.5 million. Most of these dollars are then

spent within the region.

Whistler has a thriving night life with more non-skiers

filling the bars and clubs than skiers. The après scene

has been described as legendary with DJ's and bands

from Vancouver and beyond.

# 🌐 Geography

40 kilometres away from the Pacific Ocean, settled in the valley of the Coastal Mountains lies Whistler, a picturesque "Village" only 2 hours (or 140 kilometres) for one of Canada's largest metropolises, Vancouver, along the Sea to Sky Highway between Squamish and Pemberton with five access points along the way.

If traveling by car in the winter season, keep in mind that like all mountain highway routes, weather conditions change rapidly. All visitors who fly in touch down at Vancouver International Airport (YVR) which is a short drive to the United States border.

# 🌐 Weather & Best Time to Visit

Whistler is a popular destination in the summer for hiking, biking, and many water sports like fishing and canoeing.

If you like to golf, Whistler also have champion courses designed by star designers like Arnold Palmer. With the longest skiing and snowboarding season in all of North America, winter visitors can also enjoy snowmobiling, snowshoeing and skating. You can enjoy all types of activities year round at this top notice resort.

Whistler boasts over 200 trails and 37 lifts with its' longest run 11 kilometres. This means that you can ski or snowboard for days on different terrains and areas of the mountain. The average snowfall per year is 39.1 feet (11.9 metres) and due to the coastal proximity, the temperatures rarely dips below -10 degrees Celsius. The average daily temperatures in the winter (December to February) are 5 degrees Celsius and ranges from 21 to 27 degrees Celsius in summer months with August being the warmest. Due to its location within the forests, rain can be overwhelming in the lower elevations, but rain in the valley means more snow on the hills for adventure-seekers to take advantage of.

If visiting in the fall, a must do is hiking the ancient cedar trails. There are some remarkable trees and lots of mushrooms, like Morals and Chanterelles, growing in the area. The hike takes approximately 3 hours in total but is well worth it because of the beautiful changing colors of the season. To access this hiking area, take the turn-off at Cougar Mountain and drive approximately 15 minutes up the gravel road.

## Sights & Activities: What to See & Do

# 🌐 Peak 2 Peak Gondola

You don't necessarily have to be a skier or snowboard to

enjoy a ride on the signature red gondolas. From inside

the safely enclosed space, you will have stunning views of

the sky fields, mountains and Whistler village so don't

forget your camera.

Peak 2 Peak also have a viewing gallery where you can learn about how the machinery works and watch it in action. And at the top, enjoy breath-taking views while dining at a full-service restaurant. The lift span that runs from mountain to mountain is the longest unsupported in the world at 3.024 kilometres (1.88 miles) and is the highest of its' kind, reaching elevations of 436 metres (1417 feet).

Ticket prices are $48.95 for an adult $41.95 for youth and seniors and $24.95 for children. If you book 4 days in advance, the price per ticket is reduced by a few dollars. Your ticket includes a gondola ride from the village up the Peak 2 Peak gondola, unlimited crossing on the gondola for the day, the viewing gallery, videos in the Alpine Theatre, and the 2010 Olympic Games display at the Roundhouse Lodge. The gondola operates daily from 9 am to 3 pm and is open year-round and is suitable for all ages and abilities.

www.whistler.com/gondola/

4545 Whistler Way,

Whistler, BC, Canada, V0N 1B4

1-800-766-7449

# 🌍 Olympic Park

Whistler Sliding Area, Olympic Park and the Athletes' Centre are three venues that were used in the Winter Olympic and Paralympic Games in 2010.

The parks' trail system has 27 trails for all levels from beginner to intermediate and 6 kilometres of those trails are lit. This is one of the largest Nordic areas in North

# WHISTLER TRAVEL GUIDE

America with stunning scenery. Facilities at the Olympic Park include the Day Lodge & Visitors Centre where you can purchase passes and pick up rental equipment, Brandywine Café where you can grab some lunch or have fondue for 2 (Wednesdays only). The Ski Play Zone is the Olympic Parks newest addition and is used mainly by school groups and clubs. Toboggan Hill is best for families and young children but helmets are required and can be rented at the Day Lodge. The Neverland Trail is a 3.8 kilometre cross-country skiing trail for beginners or those with no experience.

Whistler Olympic Park is open 7 days a week in the winter season (November to April) and the summer season (May to September). Monday, Tues, Thursday and Friday 9 am to 4:30 pm Wednesday open late from 9 am to 9 pm and weekends from 8:30 am to 4:30 pm (in the winter) and 10 am to 4:30 pm daily (in the summer). In the summer months, admission to the park is $10 (including tax) per vehicle or $5 for motorcycles. With all paid admissions, you will receive a $5 coupon towards experience biathlon. In the winter months, if you would like to ski Callaghan, the daily cost for an adult is $23.50 and $13.50 for youth. A family pass (maximum 4 people/2 adults) is $60.50. Snowshoeing is $14.00 per adult $7.00 per youth or $35.00 for a family. But if just some sightseeing and tobogganing is more your thing, the cost is $10.00 per vehicle. However, if you want to save a little bit of money, 10% off is available for Nordic skiing and snowshoeing midweek.

There is also a biathlon shooting area where visitors can shoot a .22 rifle at targets used in the biathlon during the 2010 Olympic Games. You will be under supervision and a staff member will walk you through how to operate a gun.  It is $10.00 for 5 bullets and $5.00 for an additional magazine of 5 bullets.

www.whistlerolympicpark.com

5 Callaghan Valley Road,

Whistler, BC, Canada V0N 1B8

1-604-964-0060

# 🌐 Whistler Blackcomb's Coca-Cola® Tube Park

Tube day or night down 1000 feet of sliding area and no special equipment or training is necessary.  There are multiple lanes for the whole family to enjoy and a conveyor will take you back to the top.

Something to take into consideration when heading to the Coca-Cola® Tube Park is that children under 12 years of age must be accompanied by an adult.  Children must be at least 36 inches tall to ride in the park and children between 36 and 41 inches may use the 2 available child lanes from the halfway point.

The park is open 12 pm to 8 pm weekdays and 11 am to 8 pm on weekends with some holiday exceptions.

4545 Blackcomb Way,

Whistler, BC, Canada V0N 1B4

1-604-932-3434

# Whistler Museum

If you are looking to get out of the cold or whether you just need a rest from skiing, the Whistler Museum has plenty of interactive exhibits to entertain the whole family. You

can even have your picture taken holding a real Olympic

torch. The display showcases 13 of the uniforms and

gear worn by athletes' of the Olympic and Paralympic

Games.

The museum tells the story of Whistlers' journey up to the

Olympic Games with stories and artifacts about the

people that made it happen. The museum displays

artifacts from many eras including Whistler's natural

environment, skiing history and the hippie and squatter

days and holds three collections: artifacts, archives and

research with important objects from the early pioneer

days.

There are many educational programs available at

Whistler Museum and in June, July and August you can

# WHISTLER TRAVEL GUIDE

take a walking tour called the Valley of Dreams where you will learn unique facts about the history of Whistler. The tours are about 1 hour long and start at 1 pm and leave from the Whistler Village Information Centre. These tours are by donation.

Open year-round 11 am to 5 pm daily. Adult admission is $7.50 Students/Seniors $6.00 Youth $4.00 and children under 6 years are free or a family (4-6 people) is $20.00. The Whistler Museum is located behind the Whistler Public Library in the heart of the village. If parking under the library, keep in mind that it is pay parking.

www.whistlermuseum.org

4333 Main Street,

Whistler, BC, Canada V0N 1B4

1-604-932-2019

# 🌎 Whistler Bungee

This fun and exciting sport received a 5 star rating from over 94 reviews on Trip Advisor but has also been voted by locals as the most extreme sport in Whistler. This adrenaline filled jump is 160 feet (50 metres) high over the Cheakamus River that is glacial fed and you are surrounded by old forest growth and basalt column cliffs.

Whistler bungee has a perfect safety record since opening in 2002. You have the option of jumping alone or tandem and they are wheelchair equip making this truly a sport anyone can try. There are three main ways to jump including using a chest harness, which is more

# WHISTLER TRAVEL GUIDE

comfortable and keeps you in an upright position, the

ankle harness, which is the most traditional way to jump

as you fall head first towards the river below and tandem,

for those too scared to jump.


They are located 15 minutes from Whistler village and

open every day, all year round in any weather condition.

Pre-booking is required and you need to arrive 15 minutes

before your scheduled jump time.  Open 12 pm to 5pm

Monday to Friday and 11 am to 5 pm Saturday and

Sunday. 1st time jumpers pay $130.00 (transportation

included) but if you have jumped at Whistler Bungee

before, the cost is $80 as you are considered a member

(transportation fee $10.00).  Discount pricing is available

for groups of 10 or more.  Transportation leaves from

Whistler Bungee's village office located on the Village

Stroll.  All spectators that require transportation must pay a $10.00 fee.  All jumpers receive a free t-shirt.  A

professional photographer is on-site and available to

capture your experience.  Pricing is available on-site.

www.whistlerbungee.com

The sales and booking office is located in the Eagle

Lodge.

19-4314 Main Street,

Whistler, BC, Canada V0N 1B4

1-877-938-9333

# 🌎 Whistler Mountain Bike Park

This bike park is gravity-assisted and has over 4900

vertical feet of biking with 3 zones (gentle cruising through

the forest, tight and twisty tracks and steep slopes with

drop offs) and over 60 trails. There is also the Air Dome; an 8400 square foot covered indoor bike training facility. This is a safe environment with foam pits and wooden ramps.

Full face helmets, gloves and biking armour are recommended, as well as full suspension bikes. Hours of operation vary per season but the Whistler Mountain Bike Park is generally open from May to October. The bike park is free to ride but a lift ticket is required to reach the top of the mountain. The cost for a 1 day pass is $61.00 for adults $53.00 for youth/seniors and $35 for children. All users must sign a waiver. Bike rentals are available at G1 Rentals (inside the Village Gondola Building) or the Demo Centre (at Carlton Lodge). The Air Dome is open various times throughout the year so be sure to check the website for details. Cost of using the Air Dome for a 3 hour session is $19.05. Rental bikes are available for

$25.00 and include a helmet.

www.bike.whistlerblackcomb.com

4545 Blackcomb Way,

Whistler, BC, Canada V0N 1B4

1-866-218-9690

# 🌐 Alexander Falls

Located just 40 minutes from Whistler in Callaghan

Valley, this 141 foot (43 metre) waterfall is open year

round. There is a viewing platform directly across from

the crashing falls or if you want more adventure, there is a

trail (level: difficult) that leads both to the top of the falls

and the bottom. There are a number of picnic areas

located in clearings and don't forget to read the

information board as there are a number of great pictures and stories.

Once you leave the highway and head into the mountains on a 10 minute drive, there may be sightings of bears as they like to eat the grass that grows along the side of the road. All the platforms and picnic areas where designed and constructed before the Olympic Games and there is a café and visitors centre, as well as, this location is connected to Whistler's Olympic Park but the gates are only open during regular business hours. Hours of operation during the summer are 10 am to 4:30 pm daily and during the winter 9 am to 4:30 pm weekdays.

This area was largely used as a logging area and there are a number of logging roads used by campers but they are bad and in disrepair so be on the cautionary side.

Keep in mind that the parking area at Alexander Falls is free but no camping or overnight stays are allowed. Dogs are allowed in all of the Callaghan Valley but be aware and cautious of wildlife.

www.whistlerhiatus.com

Callaghan Lake Provincial Park,

Whistler, BC, Canada

# Brandywine Falls

The Brandywine Falls trails are easy and the 2 kilometre hike takes approximately 30 minutes roundtrip. The falls are 66 metres and drop from an abrupt cliff. These falls are easy to locate as you will see signs along the Sea to Sky Highway, approximately 25 minutes from Squamish. Once you pull into the large parking area, it is a 1 kilometre hike over and along the Cheakamus River.

There are picnic areas and pit toilets but no other

facilities. www.whistlerhiatus.com

# 🌐 Shannon Falls

Shannon Falls is the third largest waterfall in British

Columbia at 335 metres (1105 feet).  Shannon Falls

Provincial Park is a popular tourist spot for picnicking. The

trails are well-maintained and the network lets you explore

among the trees and old stumps.  There is a large parking

area, washrooms and an information centre all located at

the falls.

The best time to visit is in the spring when the snow has

melted as it makes for a dramatic raging waterfall. From

the falls, you can take a steep 7 to 10 kilometre roundtrip

hike that takes you over the top of Stawamus Chief where

you will get a stunning view of Squamish, Howe Sound and many mountain peaks.

www.tourismsquamish.com/attractions/shannon-falls-provincial-park

# 🌐 Nairn Falls

The hiking along and to Nairn Falls is easy with well-worn trails. Allow about 1 hour to complete the 2.4 kilometre roundtrip hike. There are several picnic areas along the trail so don't forget to bring a lunch or if you want an overnight adventure, the park boasts a large camping area along the Green River. From the viewing platform, you can watch the chaotic green water crash through several areas and drop in 10 to 20 metre sections, for a total of 60 metres in height.

There is also another hiking trail that takes you away from the falls and leads to One Mile Lake. It is a 2 kilometre trail but you can enjoy swimming once you get there.

Nairn Falls is a quick drive, only 20 minutes from Whistler. The trail to the falls is open year round even with the large amount of snowfall in the winter. The campground is open May to September and can accommodate up to 94 vehicles. The cost for camping is $18 per party per night. Dogs are welcome but bikes are not. There is a hand-operated water pump and pit toilets available, along with picnic tables.

www.whistlerhiatus.com

# 🌐 Squamish

Squamish is 59.7 kilometres from Whistler, approximately a 47 minute drive and has been named the "Outdoor Recreation Capital of Canada." Some of the activities in this area include mountain biking, rock climbing, horseback riding, rafting and numerous other adventure laden activities including skiing. Squamish has also become popular for its' vibrant art scene and has the second highest number of artists as residents in all of Canada.

October is a great time to visit Squamish as the Farmer's Market is open and you will be able to purchase food and local arts, plus the Magic Pumpkin Train is operational and is a fun family event. Squamish has a number of great attractions such as the West Coast Railway Heritage Park and Britannia Mine Museum. If you just want some good laughs and good times then check out Whistle Punk Hallow Adventure Golf.

www.tourismsquamish.com

# Pemberton

Pemberton is a 29 minute drive from Whistler (33.7 kilometres).  The town sits 8000 feet below Mount Currie and is home to 2369 residents.  Before the settlers, this area was home to the Salish tribe.  The valley is known for its seed potatoes and has been nickname "Spud Valley."  World-class recreation is available in Pemberton, from hiking and biking to golf, gliding and jet boating.

Drop by the Pemberton Visitors Centre to discover all the Pemberton has to offer.

www.pemberton.ca

## Budget Tips

##  Accommodation

## Market Pavilion

Rooms start at approximately $85 per night (in the off season). This hotel is located beside Marketplace mall so there are plenty of cafés, shops, restaurants and other services just out your door.

This location is only an 8 minute walk from ski lifts and free shuttle service is available close to this location. The building has secure parking for vehicles and bicycles, as well as, an equipment storage area. There is a restaurant on site and a hot-tub in the common area. Rooms are clean, comfortable and homey.

4368 Main Street,

Whistler, BC, Canada V0N 1B4

# Glacier Lodge

Rooms start at approximately $89 per night (in the off season). This hotel is located in the upper village at the base of Blackcomb Mountain. It is a ski-in ski-out location with access to shops and restaurants. In the summer, the farmer's market is right outside or you can stroll across the street to the grocery store. The hotel features an outdoor pool (heated) and two hot-tubs, plus free internet access. The Ciao Thyme Bistro and Fitzsimmons Pub are on-site. Keep in mind that this is a 100% non-smoking hotel. There is 24 hour front desk service and a fitness centre. Parking for either vehicle or bicycle is secured, as well as, equipment storage.

4573 Chateau Boulevard,

Whistler, BC, Canada

# HI-Whistler Hostel

If value for your money is what you seek, stay at this property. HI-Whistler was built in 2010 to accommodate athletes during the Olympics. Because of this, the building boasts amenities and rooms that rival some four-star hotels. There are both private rooms and dorm-style rooms available. There is a café, Cheaky's, which is on-site that serves beer, wine and specialty coffee, and serves ups fresh homemade meals, as well as, snacks. Meet other skiers and snowboarders while you relax in the TV lounge or while playing a game of pool. Some unique features to these accommodations include bike hire and book exchange. This location is a bit of a distance from the village but a $2.50 bus ride is easily accessible. Prices are approximately $37 per night in the dorm-style room that sleeps four people or $67.50 for a private room.

1035 Legacy Way,

Whistler, BC, Canada

www.hihostels.ca

# Aava Whistler Hotel

This accommodation has been labelled "chic" and "contemporary". With only a 5 minute walk to the lifts and situated at the edge of the village where all the action takes place, this location is affordable and convenient. Many standard amenities apply to this hotel including a heated year-round outdoor pool and Keurig coffee machines in some rooms. Pets are allowed but for a small fee. Room starts at approximately $122.00 per night.

4005 Whistler Way,

Whistler, BC, Canada V0N 1B4

1-604-932-2522

www.aavawhistlerhotel.com

# Chateau Luise Inn

Another great way to stay at Whistler is in a bed and breakfast accommodation. This three-story, eight room inn is only a short 10-minute walk to the village and all the offered attractions. In the summer, this location has colorful flowers bursting from the balconies and in the surrounding gardens. It is a quiet and relaxing place for guests to unwind after a long day. The fireside lounge can provide you with much need down time; you could soak in the whirlpool or steam in the sauna. Prices start at approximately $129.00 per night.

7461 Ambassador Crescent,

Whistler, BC, Canada

1-800-665-1998

www.chateauluisewhistlerinn.com

# 🌐 Restaurants, Cafés & Bars

## Dusty's Bar & BBQ

If you love BBQ then "put the wild back into your west".

Dusty's was the original place locals went to drink and

party the night away while enjoying its' rustic decor. The

seating is picnic tables and the wood is reclaimed from

the original building. This place is lively and is known for

its' après, Caesars and live bands. The team working in

the kitchen cooking up your BBQ are truly a team of

professionals. They toured 30 restaurants to find the best

of the best and have come up with secret spice rubs and

sauces so delicious you'll be licking your fingers. If

visiting in the spring, outside seating is ideal because the

sun hits the seating area late into the day. Dusty's is

open 11am until late. The restaurant is affordable

(pitchers of beer only $12.00 and half-price Tuesdays)

and offers menu choices for those we are vegetarian as well as a children's menu.

2040 London Lane,

Whistler, BC, Canada V0N 1B2

1-604-905-2171

# Dirk & Bernie

If you enjoy a good cup of java, this is the place as they have over 45 different coffees to choose from. This is where you can get the perfect espresso in a diner-style restaurant with all –day breakfast and home-style cooked meals. The burgers at Dirk & Bernie are huge and the prices are very reasonable. Try the famous "Grizzly" burger if you want an authentic and large meal. Open Monday to Sunday 8 am to 3 pm.

4557 Blackcomb Way,

Whistler, BC, Canada

1-604-962-0606

www.dirkandbernie.com

# Hot Buns Bakery

The entrance to this sweet spot is on Sunrise Alley and whether you visit at the beginning of your day or at the end, you will enjoy some delicious eats.  Try the cinnamon buns or the pain au chocolat (known to be the best in town).  With its stone floors and simple wood furnishings, this bakery feels like you are sitting in a rural town somewhere in France sipping lattes. Grab their daily cinnamon bun special 6 buns for $2.25 Open 7 days a week from 7:30 am to 10:30 pm

4232 Village Stroll,

Whistler, BC, Canada V0N 1B0

1-604-932-6883

www.hotbuns.moonfruit.com

# La Brasserie des Artistes

Average meals but excellent views of the mountains from
the patio under yellow umbrellas; this bistro is located in
the square with a perfect vantage point to take in the
street entertainment and people watching. The décor is
interesting and eclectic and meals arrive quickly. The
steaks, burgers and breakfasts are all at reasonable
prices from $12.00 to $22.00. This is a popular spot,
known as "The Brass", for après ski and the crowd usually
lingers until midnight but getting a table doesn't usually
take too long. Grab some friends or family and enjoy a
big plate of nachos.

Village Stroll,

Whistler, BC, Canada V0N 1B0

1-604-932-3569

www.labrass.moonfruit.com

# Sushi Village

The place is buzzing with après ski and late night diners as they offer family-style hot pots, rolls, sashimi and tempera. This is a great spot to socialize and enjoy sake or try their sake margaritas. Three excellent reasons to dine at this hotspot include fresh food, friendly service and the owner, Mikito, loves the restaurant, loves Whistler and he loves life.

Sushi village imports from around the world. The salmon, tuna, shrimp and snapper are all shipped in from

Vancouver twice a week.  If you get a chance to sit at the sushi bar, ask one of the chefs to make you one of their favorite combinations as you will not be disappointed with the flare and excitement involved in the preparation.

There are private "dining rooms" available to accommodate large groups (up to 60 people) and take-out is also available.

4272 Mountain Square,

Whistler, BC, Canada V0N 1B4

1-604-932-3330

www.sushivillage.com

# Cows Ice Cream

If treats are more your thing, head to where you can get the best ice cream served in a freshly made waffle cones. You can not walk by this location without the delicious aromas enticing you to enter. Cows opened in 1983 on Prince Edward Island and have since found its way to Whistler. They still use the traditional secret recipes that children enjoyed back in the time of Anne of Green Gables. You'll be delighted with over 35 different flavors to choose from.

There are three main factors that contribute to the success and great taste of Cows ice cream: the high butter-fat content (16%), minimal air exposure making the ice cream high density so it melts slowly, and the finest and freshest ingredients like PEI berries and imported cocoa from Holland. They also sell a selection of souvenirs like silly t-shirts and coffee mugs. Trip Advisor awarded Cows with the Certificate of Excellence in 2013 and was given a 4.5 out of 5 star rating by reviewers. Cows is ranked #17 out of 158 restaurants at Whistler.

102-4295 Blackcomb Way,

Whistler, BC, Canada V0N 1B4

1-604-938-9822

<u>www.cows.ca</u>

# Rocky Mountain Chocolate Factory

Another great place for treats is the Rocky Mountain

Chocolate Factory (founded in 1981) where you can

watch fudges being made. A must try is the apples

dipped in chocolate with marshmallows and nuts. There

are 55 locations across Canada with retail operators also

located in the United States, Japan and the United

Emirates. They are rapidly expanding due to their sweet

treats become more and more popular. This is not an

eating establishment so no table service is available.

217-4293 Mountain Square,

Whistler, BC, Canada V0N 1B4

1-604-932-4100

Open daily 9 am to 11 pm

www.rockychoc.com

# Shopping

Whistler has over 200 shops to suit everyone's taste from fashion and jewelry to camping supplies. But if there is one thing you must buy while in Whistler, it is the toque (a knit cap). The toque is said to originate with the Metis and fur traders; they would leave their nightcaps on during the chilly winter months for extra warmth.

# Rocky Mountain Soap Company

If you are seeking bath and beauty goodies, try their 100% natural products. All the ingredients used in their products can be found in nature and are used in their natural form or by extraction. The owner, Karina Birch, was featured in Chatelaine October 2012 as one of the top 100 female entrepreneurs and several products have been featured in magazines such as Canadian Living. Winter weather can dry and irritate skin so be sure to try a body butter or soap that contains cocoa butter as it has softening and protecting properties. With 29 different scents and varieties of soap, there will be a kind to please everyone in the family. Soaps starts at $5.25 per bar.

4314 Main Street,

Whistler, BC, Canada V0N 1B4

1-604-932-2009

www.rockymountainsoap.com

# Armchair Books

Looking to relax with a book while on vacation?  Pick up your copy of a bestseller or some magazines at a friendly place, Armchair Books. The also carry a large selection of guides and maps for the area, so don't forget to make a quick stop before you head out onto the trails.  There are also a number of books about wildlife and the flora and fauna in the area.  Their Facebook page is a great place to find details about upcoming events and scheduled readings.  They are open 7 days a week, 9 am to 9 pm.

4205 Village Square,

Whistler, BC, Canada V0N 1B4

1-604-932-5557

www.whistlerbooks.com

# Amos & Andes

Whistler has many shops were you can buy sweaters (from wool to cashmere) but this one is by far the best.  It is a stand-out shop because all of its sweaters are handmade. The owner has been quoted saying "I grew up on a farm wearing jeans, t-shirts and sweaters that Granny made."  Check out their Facebook page at Amos and Andes: The Whistler Sweater Shop to see the latest styles and get tips directly from Granny herself like how to fold a sweater properly (includes a link to a Youtube video).

2-4321 Village Gate,

Whistler, BC, Canada V0N 1B4

1-604-932-7202

www.whistlersweatershop.com

Know Before You Go

#  Entry Requirements

To visit Canada as a tourist you will need a valid travel document, such as a passport, a certificate of good health and a clean record with absolutely no criminal convictions. Additionally, you may be asked to convince immigration officers of strong ties with your home country, your intent to leave at the end of your stay and your means to support yourself financially for the duration of your stay. In most cases, you will also need an entry document in the form of either a visitor visa or, in the case of citizens of countries that are visa exempt, an Electronic Travel Authorization (eTA). Visitors from the USA, members of the Royal Family and French residents of St. Pierre and Miquelon are the only persons exempt from needing an eTA. In the case of family groups, each family member will need to apply separately for an Electronic Travel Authorization. Countries exempted from requiring a visa include the United Kingdom (and British Overseas Territories such as Gibraltar, Pitcairn Island, the Falkland Islands, the Cayman Islands, Montserrat, Bermuda, the British Virgin Islands, St Helena, Anguilla, the Turks and Caicos Islands), Australia, New Zealand, Belgium, the Netherlands, France, Greece, Cyprus, Austria, Germany, Denmark, Finland, Sweden, Norway, Iceland, Spain, Portugal, Switzerland, Italy, Ireland, Hungary,

Poland, the Czech Republic, Japan, Croatia, Slovenia, Slovakia, Latvia, Lithuania, Liechtenstein, Malta, Monaco, San Marino, Andorra, Samoa, Papua New Guinea, the Solomon Islands, Chile, the Republic of Korea and Singapore. A visitor's visa is valid for 6 months and you can apply to have this extended by 30 days.

# 🌐 Health insurance

Medical treatment can be expensive in Canada and the Canadian government does not offer any payment for medical treatment. There are no reciprocal agreements between Canada and the UK, the European Union or Australia regarding medical treatment. For this reason, visitors should make arrangements for sufficient health insurance to cover any medical emergencies as well as repatriation, if it is required, before leaving home. Temporary health insurance can be arranged through a Canadian agency for a period of up to 365 days, with premiums starting at between $20 and $25. When considering insurance policies, do bear in mind that some extreme outdoor sports like skiing may not be covered automatically by your policy. If you are planning to participate in activities not normally covered, you should make arrangements for additional cover.

# Travelling with Pets

When travelling with pets to Canada, the first requirement is the submission of proper travel documents. In the case of dogs, the animal will need to be inspected at the point of entry and a fee for this is levied at $30. All points of entry to Canada have an animal inspector on duty, which means that advance notification is not required.

Cats entering Canada do not need to be quarantined or microchipped, but they will need to be accompanied by a detailed rabies vaccination certificate or a health certificate stating that they are from a country recognized by Canada as rabies free. In the case of pets from the European Union, a pet passport will be accepted as alternative, provided it contains all the required details. Guide dogs and other assistance dogs are exempt from most of the restrictions that apply to other animal importations.

No import certificate is required for most reptiles and amphibians, with the exception of tortoises and turtles, in which case an application must be made a minimum of 30 days prior to import date to the Canadian Food Inspection Agency. Pet birds need to spend at least 45 days in quarantine, where a CFIA inspector will inspect their health. Application for quarantine must be made prior to your arrival in Canada. You will also need to make a declaration stating that the bird(s) have been in your possession for a minimum of 90 days and have not been in contact with other birds during that period. Birds originating from China, Vietnam, Bangladesh, Egypt, India and Indonesia are prohibited from entering Canada.

# Airports

**Toronto Pearson International Airport** (YYZ) is the busiest airport in Canada in terms of passenger traffic. Located 22.5km northwest of Toronto's downtown area, it provides access to Toronto, the capital of Ontario as well as the Golden Horseshoe, Canada's most populous region. Terminal 1, its primary terminal is one of the largest buildings of its kind in the world and its modern facilities are streamlined by the ThyssenKrupp Express Walkway, one of the fastest people-moving walkways in the world. The airport also has shops, a variety of eateries and free Wi-Fi coverage. A second airport serving Toronto is the **Billy Bishop Toronto City Airport** (YTZ), named after Canada's top flying ace from World War 1. It is located on an island in Toronto Harbour. From the airport, Toronto's CBD can be reached via a pedestrian tunnel from Eireann Quay or a scheduled ferry service. The airport falls under the Toronto Port Authority and is co-administered with the city's harbour. Besides three runways, there is also a base for seaplanes.

# WHISTLER TRAVEL GUIDE

Ontario's third major airport is the **Ottawa/Macdonald–Cartier International Airport** (YOW), the 6th busiest in Canada and 2nd busiest in the province. It serves Ottawa, but also offers connections to the bustling centers of Toronto and Montreal as well as a gateway to the Arctic.

**Vancouver International Airport** (YVR) lies on Sea Island in Richmond, about 12km from the downtown area of Vancouver City. Although planning for the airport began as early as 1929, the site first served as a Royal Canadian Air Force base during World War Two and the proposed civilian airport only became a reality after the war. As a Pacific Gateway, Vancouver International Airport provides non-stop connections to Asia and the International Terminal offers United States Border Preclearance facilities. The multi-award-winning airport welcomes visitors to Canada with a striking collection of Aboriginal art in the form of wooden sculptures and totem poles as well as the YVR Aquarium with over 800 marine species. Regular airport personnel are backed by a team of volunteers, trained to assist travellers in navigating their way through the airport. To aid the disabled, special wheelchair lifts have been installed and check-in counters have headsets for travellers with hearing disabilities. The rapid transit Sky Train connects to Vancouver's metro rail service. Vancouver International Airport also offers free Wi-Fi coverage. The second busiest airport in British Columbia is **Victoria International Airport** (YYJ), which offers access to Vancouver Island. Recently renovated, it has various features for disabled travellers, including wheel chair friendly facilities, large signage, phones with augmented transmission and relieving areas for service dogs. The airport is set in scenic surroundings and environmental management is a high priority. Several of its ground vehicles are electrically powered and there is a bicycle assembly station just outside the main terminal as well as a bike path.

**Montréal–Pierre Elliott Trudeau International Airport** (YUL), formerly known as Montréal–Dorval International Airport, is located in the suburb of Dorval, about 20km from downtown Montreal. Utilized from the 1940s, it provides access to Montreal and Quebec, but can also serve as a gateway to parts of Ontario and even Vermont and New York in the USA. Like Vancouver, it offers United States Border Preclearance facilities, making it a modern and people friendly trans border terminal. Find your way around the airport easily with the YULi smartphone app. For easy access from the airport, a shuttle bus service connects travellers to the metro service to stops at Lionel-Groulx metro station, Central Station and Berri-UQAM metro station. **Halifax Stanfield International Airport** (YHZ) provides access to the mainland of Nova Scotia as well as its nearby maritime regions. **Winnipeg James Armstrong Richardson International Airport** (YWG) first opened in 1928 and is one of Canada's oldest airports. It is located about

10km from Winnipeg's downtown area and offers access to Winnipeg and the province of Manitoba. Additionally, it also serves as a gateway to the remote northern regions. One of its original hangars has been converted to an aviation museum, where visitors can view a collection of historical bush planes as well as Canada's first helicopter.

The province of Alberta is served by two large airports. **Calgary International Airport** (YYC) offers access to its most populous city and the majestic Canadian Rocky Mountains. First opened in 1938, it has entered a transitional phase with its new facilities scheduled for opening at the end of October 2016. If you have a few hours to while away, visit the Space Port, where you can enjoy simulated space flights or view artefacts on loan from NASA. **Edmonton International Airport** (YEG) is located about 26km from downtown Edmonton and offers a gateway to the Northern part of Alberta. Both Calgary and Edmonton have United States Border Preclearance facilities. **Kuujjuaq Airport** (YVP) is located about 2.8km southwest of Kuujjuaq in Quebec and provides access to the remote Nunavik region. It is a mandatory frequency airport, which means that it does not have sufficient air traffic to warrant a control tower.

#  Airlines

Air Canada is the flag carrier and largest airline in Canada. It was founded from Trans-Canada Airlines in the 1930s, renamed in the 1960s and privatized in the 1980s, following the deregulation of Canada's air travel industry. The service flies to over 100 international and domestic destinations and is linked by codeshare agreement to 28 other international airlines, including Lufthansa, United Airlines, Aegean Airlines, EgyptAir, Jet Airways, Turkish Airlines, Singapore Airlines, Air India, Air China, All Nippon Airways and Scandinavian Airlines.

WestJet is a Canadian budget airline that was founded in the mid-1990s. Currently it is the second largest carrier in Canada, flying up to 20 million passengers annually to over 100 destinations. The airline offers no-frills service and embraces environmentally sustainable strategies. Jazz Aviation is a regional service that connects passengers to over 75 destinations in Canada and the USA. Another budget airline is Sunwing Airlines, which is based in Toronto and was recently acquired by the US tour operator, Vacation Express. Perimeter Aviation is the largest regional aircraft carrier in Manitoba and offers connections to 23 destinations in Manitoba and Ontario. It also supports the region's medical evacuation services.

Air Inuit is collectively owned by the Inuit community of Nunavik and it offers connections to domestic destinations in Quebec, Nunavut, Newfoundland and Labrador. Calm Air is a regional service that provides regional connections between the northern parts of Manitoba and Nunavut. It is based at Thompson in Manitoba. Pacific Coastal Airlines connects travellers to destinations in British Columbia. Another regional carrier serving British Columbia is the family run Orca Airways.

#  Hubs

Toronto Pearson International Airport serves as the largest hub for Air Canada, but the airline also operates hubs at Montréal–Pierre Elliott Trudeau International Airport, where it is based, Calgary International Airport and Vancouver International Airport. Additionally, it has a strong presence at the international airports of Edmonton, Halifax, Ottawa and Winnipeg. The primary hub for the budget carrier WestJet is Toronto Pearson International Airport. Its second hub is at Calgary International Airport, where it is based. WestJet also has a strong presence at Edmonton International Airport, Vancouver International Airport and Winnipeg James Armstrong Richardson International Airport. The primary base for Jazz Airline is at Halifax Stanfield International Airport.

Jazz also has hubs at Vancouver International Airport, Calgary International Airport, Toronto Pearson International Airport and Montréal–Pierre Elliott Trudeau International Airport. Winnipeg James Armstrong Richardson International Airport and Thompson Airport serve as hubs for Perimeter Aviation. Kuujjuaq Airport is the main operating base for Inuit Air. Calm Air has two primary hubs at Thompson Airport and Winnipeg James Armstrong Richardson International Airport and secondary hubs at Churchill Airport in Manitoba and Rankin Inlet in Nunavut. Vancouver International Airport serves as the main hub for Pacific Coastal Airlines and also serves as a hub for Orca Airways.

# 🌏 Money Matters

# 🌏 Currency

The currency for Canada is the Canadian Dollar, which is often fairly close in value to the US dollar. The currency is available in denominations of $5, $10, $20, $50, and $100. Coins are issued in denominations of 5c (a nickel), 10c (a dime), 25c (a quarter), $1 (a loonie) and $2 (a toonie or twoonie). In 2011, Canada introduced the more resilient polymer bank note, which will eventually replace the paper bank note. At present, older paper notes are still in circulation and both types of notes are considered legal tender.

# 🌎 Banking/ATMs

You will be able to withdraw Canadian dollars from Automatic Teller Machines across Canada, but you should expect to pay a bank fee of $2 to $5, as well as a small percentage for the foreign currency transaction. If your bank is partnered with a Canadian bank, you can save on part of the fee. Bank of America, Barclays Bank in the UK, France, Spain and several African countries, Westpac in Australia, New Zealand, Tonga, Samoa and Fiji, Deutsche Bank, BNP Paribas and affiliate bank brands and Banca Nazionale del Lavoro in Italy are partnered with Scotiabank through the Global ATM Alliance, which means that you will be able to save on some of the usual bank fees, although a percentage charge on foreign currency will still apply. Do remember to inform your bank of your travel plans before leaving home.

# 🌎 Credit Cards

Credit cards are widely accepted as legal tender across Canada. MasterCard and Visa are commonly accepted by most Canadian shops or businesses, although some travellers have reported problems with Visa in Canada. Walmart recently issued a statement that they will no longer accept Visa at their Canadian outlets, although they still accept MasterCard, American Express and Discover. Canada adapted to chip-and-pin credit card technology several years ago and you should experience no trouble using a card from the UK or European Union. Since financial institutions in Canada no longer accept liability for magnetic strip transactions, American visitors with older magnetic strips may experience difficulty using their credit cards as payment.

# Tourist Tax

At present, Ontario is the only province in Canada that has not yet introduced legislation regarding hotel tax, but a number of cities in the province, such as Toronto, voluntarily collect what is termed as a destination marketing fee of 3 percent. In Vancouver 8 percent provincial tax plus 3 percent municipal tax is levied on hotel accommodation. St Johns in Newfoundland and Labrador levies a 4 percent tax on hotel rooms, while Gros Morne levies 3 percent. In Alberta, a hotel room tax of 5 percent is levied. In Quebec the rate varies, but is usually charged at $2 or $3 or 3 to 3.5 percent per night depending on the location of the accommodation. Winnipeg in Manitoba levies 5 percent, but exempts budget accommodation and hostels. Brandon in Manitoba also levies 5 percent, while Thompson levies $3 per night. Halifax levies 2 percent tax on larger hotels. In Charlottetown in Prince Edward Island, 2 percent tax is levied on tourist accommodation. Bathurst in New Brunswick adds $2 per night for accommodation, while Miramichi, Saint John and Charlotte County levy a municipal tax for tourists of 2 percent. Around Niagara Falls, 3 percent destination marketing fee is levied.

# 🌐 Claiming Back VAT

In Canada, the tax on purchases and services varies according to province. In Alberta, British Columbia, Manitoba, Nunavut, Northwestern Territories, Saskatchewan and Yukon, a goods and services tax rate (GST) of 5 percent applies. Ontario, Nova Scotia, New Brunswick, Prince Edward Island, Newfoundland and Labrador levy the so-called harmonized sales tax (HST), which combines federal and provincial taxes. The rate of HST is 13 percent in Ontario, New Brunswick, Newfoundland and Labrador, 14 percent in Prince Edward Island and 15 percent in Nova Scotia. Quebec levies 5 percent GST plus 9.975 percent Quebec Sales Tax. In 2007, Canada replaced the existing tax rebates for tourists and non-residents with the Foreign Convention and Tour Incentive Program (FCTIP), which limits rebates to taxes paid for tour packages or conventions. You are eligible if the amount spent exceeds $200 without the tax component and the supplier/tour operator has not yet refunded you through other channels.

# 🌍 Tipping Policy

In Canada, tipping is common practice and attitudes are generally similar to the USA. It is customary to tip between 10 and 15 percent on your restaurant bill. In most cases, a service charge is not included. In bars, $0.50-$1 per drink is acceptable. If you are having pizza delivered, tip the delivery person. Tip about $2 per bag to hotel porters and tip your taxi driver 10 percent. Hairdressers should also be tipped for good service.

# 🌍 Connectivity

# 🌍 Mobile Phones

Canada's mobile phone networks are compatible with networks in the USA, but different from most other networks around the world as it favors CDMA networks, rather than the GSM networks used in most of Europe, Asia and Africa. While this may be technologically convenient for visitors from the USA, there is still the matter of roaming fees, which can be expensive, even for US tourists. Some US service providers do offer special deals for calls from Canada, or the option to limit charges and usage to a pre-set daily rate. Only three Canadian service providers provide close to nationwide coverage. They are Rogers, Telus and Bell. Wind Mobile offers coverage mainly in the urban and semi-urban areas of Canada, but partners with other networks to make up the difference. Additionally, there are a number of regional services, such as Ice Wireless, which covers parts of Inuvik, Yukon and the Northwestern Territories, MTS Mobility in Manitoba, Sasktel Mobility in Saskatchewan, Vidéotron Mobile in Ottawa and Quebec and Eastlink on Canada's Atlantic seaboard.

Canada's mobile industry is geared mainly towards locals, with contracts being preferred over prepaid options and a Canadian credit card being mandatory for the activation of most mobile deals. However, the industry is slowly changing to meet the demands of tourists. Bell is Canada's oldest telephone company, but they have moved with the times. If your main priority is staying connected to the web, your best bet will be their data only sim card, available at about $9.95. You can top-up using a Bell recharge voucher. Rogers is the Canadian carrier that is most compatible with international networks. They offer free sims for the activation with a new phone purchase, but will charge $10 for a replacement sim if you have your own device.

Once you have your sim card, you can choose from various usage plans starting at $30 or choose a pay-per-minute plan with minimum $10 top-ups and the option of data add-ons. Rogers is partnered with Fido and Chatr Mobile.

# 🌍 Dialing Code

The dialing code for Canada is +1, the same as the United States.

# 🌍 Emergency numbers

General Emergency: 911

MasterCard: 1 800 307 7309

Visa: 1 800 847 2911

# 🌍 General Information

# 🌍 Public Holidays

1 January: New Year's Day

March/April: Good Friday

1 July: Canada Day

# WHISTLER TRAVEL GUIDE

First Monday in September: Labor Day

25 December: Christmas Day


Several public holidays are only observed in certain states. The official separation of Nunavut from the North-Western Territories is celebrated in Nunavut on the 9th of July. Quebec observes Easter Monday, National Patriot's Day (on the Monday preceding 25 May) and Jean Baptiste Day, also known as Quebec Day (24 June). Victoria Day falls on the Monday on or before 24 May and it is observed in all states except New Brunswick, Nova Scotia and Prince Edward Island. In the Northwest Territories, 21 June is a Provincial holiday celebrated as National Aboriginal Day. Discovery Day is celebrated in 3 states. In Newfoundland and Labrador, it falls on the Monday closest to 24 June and in Yukon, it is commemorated on the Monday nearest to 17 August. Thanksgiving is celebrated on the second Monday in October in most states, except for New Brunswick, Newfoundland, Nova Scotia and Prince Edward Island. Remembrance Day is observed in most states as a statutory holiday, with the exception of Manitoba, Nova Scotia, Ontario and Quebec. While special events like Mother's Day, Valentine's Day, Father's Day and Halloween are widely observed, they are not holidays. Although not a statutory holiday, Civic Day is observed on the first Monday of August in Alberta, British

Columbia, New Brunswick, Nunavut, Ontario and Saskatchewan.

# 🌎 Time Zones

Canada is divided into six different time zones. Newfoundland Standard Time is used in the areas of Newfoundland and the south-eastern tip of Labrador. It can be calculated as Greenwich Mean Time/Co-ordinated Universal Time (GMT/UTC) -3 hours and 30 minutes in winter and -2 hours and 30 minutes in summer. Atlantic Standard Time is used in most of Labrador, New Brunswick, Nova Scotia, Prince Edward Island and Quebec. It is calculated as Greenwich Mean Time/Co-ordinated Universal Time (GMT/UTC) -4 hours in winter and -3 hours in summer. Eastern Standard Time (EST) applies in most of Nunavut, Ontario and Quebec and is calculated as Greenwich Mean Time/Co-ordinated Universal Time (GMT/UTC) -5 hours in winter and -4 hours in summer. Central Standard Time (CST) is observed in Manitoba, Saskatchewan and parts of Ontario and can be calculated as Greenwich Mean Time/Co-ordinated Universal Time (GMT/UTC) -6 hours in winter and -5 hours in summer. Mountain Standard Time (MST) is observed in Alberta, the Northwestern Territories, eastern communities in British Columbia, Lloydminster in Saskatchewan and Kugluktuk Cambridge Bay in Nunavut. It is calculated as

Greenwich Mean Time/Co-ordinated Universal Time (GMT/UTC) -7 hours in winter. Pacific Standard Time (PST) applies in Yukon and most of British Columbia and can be calculated as Greenwich Mean Time/Co-ordinated Universal Time (GMT/UTC) -8 hours in winter and -7 hours in summer.

# 🌎 Daylight Savings Time

Clocks are set forward one hour at 01.00am on the last Sunday of March and set back one hour at 01.00am on the last Sunday of October for Daylight Savings Time. Most of the province of Saskatchewan (except Creighton and Denare Beach) does not observe Daylight Savings Time and neither do Pickle Lake, New Osnaburgh and Atikokan in Ontario, Quebec's North Shore, Southampton Island in Nunavut and Creston in British Columbia.

# 🌎 School Holidays

In Canada, the academic year runs from mid September to the latter part of June. There is a two week winter break in December and a two week spring break in March. In most provinces, the summer holidays begin on the last Saturday of

June, although Quebec factors in the public holiday on 24 June. Schools begin again on the Tuesday after Labor Day.

# 🌏 Trading Hours

In Canada, trading hours are regulated at provincial level. In British Columbia, Alberta, and Saskatchewan, as well as Yukon, Northwestern Territories and Nunavut, there are no legislation prohibiting trade at any particular time, but trading hours will usually vary according to the area and the type of business. Common trading hours are from 10am to 6pm from Mondays to Saturdays, with shops also being open from noon to 5pm on Sundays. At larger city malls you can expect late trade on Thursdays, Fridays and Saturdays. In urban areas, there will usually be a pharmacy and convenience store trading 24 hours and some fast food outlets may also trade round the clock. Post Office hours may vary, according to the location of the outlet. In Quebec, shopping hours are set at 9.30am to 5.30pm from Mondays to Wednesdays, 9.30am to 9pm on Thursdays and Fridays, 9.30am to 5pm on Saturdays and 10am to 5pm on Sundays. In Nova Scotia, shops are closed on Remembrance Day, whereas in Manitoba, Quebec, Ontario, New Brunswick and Prince Edward Island, shops are closed on most major public holidays, including Remembrance Day. In those states, Sunday trading is also restricted.

# 🌍 Driving Policy

Canadians drive on the right side of the road. If you have a valid driver's license in your own country, you should be permitted to drive in Canada, but it may be advised that you apply for an International Driving Permit, which will include a translation of your licence in English and French. The minimum driving age is 16. To drive in Canada, car insurance is compulsory and you will be required to organize a policy that provides adequate cover for your age group and driving experience. If renting a car, check that car insurance is including in your rental agreement. All ten provinces in Canada have legislation restricting the use of mobile phones while driving and requires you to use a hands free kit. Speed limits are given in kilometers. In Canada, the speed limits are set at 110km per hour for multiple lane highways, 80km per hour for 2-lane highways, 60km per hour for urban and suburban roads, between 40 and 50km per hour for residential roads and 30km per hour for school zones.

# 🌍 Drinking Policy

In Canada, legislation regarding the sale and consumption of alcohol is set at the provincial level. In most provinces, the minimum drinking age is 19, with the exception of Alberta, Manitoba and Quebec, where you can legally drink from 18 years of age. An old law dating back to 1928 prohibits Canadians from transporting alcohol across provincial and national boundaries without permission from the provincial liquor control board. Do bear this in mind, if you are planning to travel through several provinces or territories with your own supply of beer or wine. It is against the law. Of the provinces, Quebec has the most relaxed liquor laws and allows alcohol sales from regular grocery stores.

# 🌍 Smoking Policy

Smoking legislation is determined at provincial level in Canada. All provinces adopted some form of restriction on smoking in public places and work spaces in the period between 2003 and 2008. In Nunavut, which has the highest percentage of smokers, it is illegal to smoke within 3 metres of a building's entrance. In Toronto, you may not smoke within 9 metres of a building's entrance. In Manitoba, Quebec, Saskatchewan, British Columbia, Nova Scotia, Ontario, New Brunswick,

Newfoundland and Labrador, it is illegal to smoke in a vehicle if minors under the age of 16 are passengers. Alberta also restricts the type of outlets that are allowed to sell cigarettes.

#  Electricity

Electricity: 110 volts

Frequency: 60 Hz

Canada uses electricity sockets similar to those found in the USA, with two flat prongs or blades arranged parallel to each other. These are compatible with Type A and Type B plugs. You will also find that appliances from the UK or Europe which were designed to accommodate a higher voltage will not function as effectively in Canada. While a converter or transformer should be able to adjust the voltage, you may still experience some performance degradations with the type of devices that are sensitive to variations in frequency as the Canada uses 60 Hz, instead of the 50 Hz which is common in Europe and the UK.

# Food & Drink

Breakfast in Canada can be a hearty mix of fried bacon, pork sausage, eggs, deep-fried potatoes, toast and pancakes, but continental twists such as French toast and pastries are equally popular, as is cereal. Lunch is generally a light meal such as sandwiches, salads or soup. Traditionally meat is central to the Canadian dinner. Canada also has its own range of tempting sweets and confectionaries. Maple syrup is a staple ingredient of various cookies and pastries. Canadian chocolate bars include the Coffee Crisp, made of coffee flavored wafers smothered in milk chocolate and the Nanaimo Bar, a British Columbian snack with with a rich buttery filling sandwiched between two slices of chocolate. The Beaver's Tail is a lump of deep-fried dough sprinkled with sugar and cinnamon. Poutine is a simple fast food that originated in Quebec and consists of French fries, smothered in cheese and gravy. Sometimes chicken, bacon, sausage, ground beef or other meat is added. Another French-Canadian favorite is Tourtière, or meat pies, usually made of beef, veal or pork. If you have trouble choosing between pizza and pasta, then the Pizza-ghetti is for you. It combines half a pizza with a helping of Spaghetti Bolognaise.

Canadian coffee culture embraces the simplicity of Tim Horton, the country's most popular chain of coffee and doughnut shops, but in recent years, tastes have grown somewhat more sophisticated and cosmopolitan. Bottled glacier water is available across Canada. Coke, Pepsi and Diet Coke are the best selling soft drinks, but for a taste of local flavor, try Jones Soda, which features a range of tastes including green apple, bubblegum, strawberry lime, crushed melon and even peanut butter and jelly. Some of their limited editions include pumpkin pie and poutine flavored soft drinks. Ginger ale is a Canadian invention and another Canadian favorite is clamato juice, a combination of clam chowder and tomato juice, which is combined with vodka to produce the Bloody Caesar, the country's signature cocktail.

Beer is Canada's favorite alcoholic beverage and Budweiser from across the border, its top selling brand. Canadian beer drinkers love to experiment, which accounts for the popularity of craft beers and also the introduction of ice beer amidst fierce rivalry by two of Canada's top beer brewers, Labatt and Molson. Both brands are based in the province of Quebec which has a lively beer brewing tradition and hosts two annual beer festivals, one in Quebec City and one in Montreal. Canadians also produce ice wine, a sweet dessert wine and rye whiskey, of which the award-winning Canadian Club and Crown Royal are its most representative brands.

 # Useful Websites

http://wikitravel.org/en/Canada

https://www.attractionscanada.com/

http://www.frontier-canada.co.uk/

http://www.canadianbucketlist.com/

http://transcanadahighway.com/

http://www.tour-guide-canada.com/

http://www.thecanadaguide.com/

Made in the USA
San Bernardino, CA
09 July 2016